INSTANT TEEN™

JUST ADD NUTS

By
Haruka Fukushima

HAMBURG // LONDON // LOS ANGELES // TOKYO

Instant Teen: Just Add Nuts
created by Haruka Fukushima

Translation - Yoohae Yang
English Adaptation - Jeannie Andersen
Retouch and Lettering - Samantha Yamasaki and Bowen Park
Production Artist - Jose Macasocol, Jr.
Copy Editor - Suzanne Waldman
Cover Design - Gary Shum

Editor - Jodi Bryson
Digital Imaging Manager - Chris Buford
Pre-Press Manager - Antonio DePietro
Production Managers - Jennifer Miller and Mutsumi Miyazaki
Art Director - Matt Alford
Managing Editor - Jill Freshney
VP of Production - Ron Klamert
Editor-in-Chief - Mike Kiley
President and C.O.O. - John Parker
Publisher and C.E.O. - Stuart Levy

A Manga

TOKYOPOP Inc.
5900 Wilshire Blvd. Suite 2000
Los Angeles, CA 90036

E-mail: info@TOKYOPOP.com
Come visit us online at www.TOKYOPOP.com

ISBN: 1-59532-148-9

First TOKYOPOP printing: March 2005
10 9 8 7 6 5 4 3 2 1
Printed in the USA

...BY EATING SOME MIRACLE NUTS...

WOW!!

...SHE SUDDENLY TRANSFORMS INTO A YOUNG WOMAN WITH A NICE BODY.

NATSUMI KAWASHIMA
SHE'S A NORMAL FIFTH GRADER. SHE DREAMS OF BECOMING A SEXY YOUNG WOMAN AND ONE DAY...

DR. MORINOMIYA
SHE'S A GENETIC ENGINEERING GENIUS WHO INVENTED THE MIRACLE NUTS.

THESE ARE THE NUTS INVENTED BY DR. MORINOMIYA. YOU BECOME AN ADULT SUDDENLY BY EATING THESE NUTS.

ASUMA YONEYAMA
HE'S NATSUMI'S CHILD-HOOD FRIEND AND LIVES NEXT DOOR. NATSUMI ALWAYS TROUBLES HIM....

Story so far of
✳✳✳ **"Instant Teen: Just Add Nuts"** ✳✳✳✳

☆ NATSUMI IS A NORMAL ELEMENTARY SCHOOL GIRL. SHE DREAMS OF BECOMING A SEXY WOMAN SOMEDAY! ONE DAY, SHE ATE MIRACLE NUTS BY MISTAKE AND...WOW! SHE TRANSFORMED INTO A SEXY WOMAN!

THE MIRACLE NUTS WERE INVENTED BY DR. MORINOMIYA. THEY SPEED UP THE GROWTH PROCESS IN LIVING THINGS. BUT THE NUTS ARE STILL IN THE EXPERIMENTAL STAGE. WHEN NATSUMI SUDDENLY TURNS BACK INTO A CHILD, EVERYONE AROUND NATSUMI IS IN TROUBLE!

NATSUMI WAS CHOSEN TO BE A MODEL, SO SHE AND ASUMA WENT TO THE ISLANDS TO PARTICIPATE IN A PHOTO SHOOT. NATSUMI ALMOST MARRIED A SUPER RICH PLAYER NAMED BILL WENTZ! BUT SHE TURNED INTO A CHILD WHILE SHE WAS RUNNING AWAY FROM BILL'S BODY-GUARDS AND WAS SAVED! ASUMA IS THE ONLY ONE WHO CAN SAVE NATSUMI WHEN SHE'S IN MAJOR TROUBLE.

HEY! STOP IT! ♡

NOT RIGHT NOW. ♡

IT'S FINE. JUST A KISS. ♡

HEY! I SAID NO!

UMMMMM. ♡

KAWARA COMMUNITY NEWS SUNNY LAND 8

☑ **MECHANICAL PENCIL AND ME**

I found colored lead and I bought 4 colors even though they were kind of expensive!

The bag is opened...

...and I was holding them upside down.

It can't be...

Stationery

Well, what will I use these new color leads for?

I'm home!

There is only one packet of lead?! I must have dropped the other ones somewhere!!

Stationery

That's what you get for spending so much money on junk!

※ After that, I went to look for them... but I couldn't find them because it was already nighttime.

WERE YOU SURPRISED?

DR. MORINOMIYA IMPROVED THE NUTS FOR ME, SO I CAN TRANSFORM FASTER.

WHAT THE HECK ARE YOU THINKING TRANSFORM-ING HERE ALL OF A SUDDEN?!

It hurts!

THE GENETIC ENGINEERING GENIUS DR. MORINOMIYA INVENTED THE MIRACLE NUTS.

BY EATING THE NUTS...

...THE NORMAL SCHOOL-GIRL NATSUMI KAWASHIMA...

WHAT THE HECK?!

I'M NOT A KID ANYMORE

ONE

Hello! This is Haruka Fukushima.

This is volume three of Instant Teen: Just Add Nuts.

Thank you very much for purchasing the comic!

HAPPY LUCK!

This story is already finished in the comic magazine. (Crying Face: La la la...) But we are still waiting for the final volume of the manga to be released. I hope you are looking forward to it, too!

Let's run together!

I am full of spirit!

I MUST FINISH THESE PHYSICAL EXAMS ASAP AND LOOK FOR NATSUMI.

REALLY?

AND SHE'S ALSO REALLY PRETTY!

THAT FEMALE DOCTOR IS SOOO HOT!

NEXT PERSON!

I want to see her

Me, too!

YES!

BUST 33"!

WAIST 22"!

HIPS 33"!

EEEEEEEEK!

I WARNED YOU TO BE CAREFUL!

WHAT DID YOU SAY?! DR. NANAO FOUND OUT WHO YOU ARE?!

IT'S NOT EXACTLY LIKE HE FOUND OUT.

HE KNEW ABOUT ME AND THE NUTS...

...AND DR. MORINOMIYA, TOO.

KAWARA COMMUNITY NEWS SUNNY LAND 9

OKAYAMA DIALECT AND ME

One day, I was talking to other manga artists, Asumi Hara and Eiko Ohuchi from "Nakayoshi"...

Huh?

Serious

What do you mean by "yoh-sen"?

...I can't do it...

That means YOH...

YOH-SEN means...

Wa... wait, Haruka!

Yoh-sen*!

*"Yoh-sen literally means "I can't do such a thing."

Wa ha ha!

YOH-SEN means YOH-SEN!

Wait! Haruka!!

Ha ha ha!

Yo... yoh...

...yoh means...

What's YOH?

YOH ...?

YOH...?

X: Lately, I tend to use my dialect for everyday conversation.

Ohuchi   Hara

DON'T GET MAD SO EASILY.

I'M TRYING TO GET A GIFT FOR MOTHER'S DAY.

WHAT THE HECK ARE YOU DOING BY TRANSFORMING INTO AN ADULT SO EARLY IN THE MORNING?

WHAT KIND OF PERFORMANCE ARE YOU GONNA DO IN THAT COSTUME?

PERFOR- MANCE? WHAT ARE YOU TALKING ABOUT?

DO YOU HAVE ANY SPECIAL SKILLS?

Anniversary of Mother's Day

Date and Time: Mother's Day 10:00 a.m.

Place: Alice Garden Special Event Stage

Requirements: Women who live in the town and are older than 16 years old

Performance: All participants are required to showcase their talent.

Judges: Owners of the shopping mall

Yeah!

I'LL APPLY FOR THIS BEAUTY CONTEST...

LOOK!

WHAT DO YOU MEAN?

LOOK HERE! IT SAYS THAT ALL THE PARTICIPANTS HAVE TO SHOWCASE ONE OF THEIR BEST SKILLS!

...AND WIN A SPA DAY!

WHAT ?!

DON'T YOU MEAN... IF YOU WIN?

OKAY!

Ah!

Ah!

Let me check you out! ♥

YOU LOOK TOTALLY DIFFERENT.

WHY COULDN'T I WIN OVER SUCH A BEAUTIFUL WOMAN...?

I'M SO IMPRESSED WITH THE "JAPANESE CACAO!"

SHE'S ONLY A LITTLE GIRL WITH SOME STUPID NUTS...

WHYYYYY??

FROM NOW ON...

...I WILL MAKE SURE TO MAKE THAT LITTLE WITCH'S LIFE MISERABLE OVER AND OVER AND OVER!

...IT IS VERY DIFFICULT TO FIX THEIR FRIENDSHIP.

TWO

Dr. Nanao, a rival of Dr. Morinomiya, suddenly appears. I like this stupid character. Natsumi is turning into a major airhead! She starts butting heads with Dr. Nanao. In this chapter, something happens to her face! It sometimes gets...

What ?!

...deformed like this and I can't help but think "What a face!" But I enjoy drawing her like that too much and can't stop! Even if she is the heroine of the story.

Redraw her face!

Yes, mom.

My manager still makes me draw her over and over! All the redraws!!

.....∩)

CLASS THREE SIXTH GRAD

THERE HE IS!

EH? WHICH ONE?

LOOK, HE IS READING A BOOK RIGHT BY THE WINDOW...

THIS ↓

WHAT KIND OF BOOK ARE YOU READING?

LET'S KEEP OUR PROMISE.

...AND WASN'T THERE AT MY GRADUATION.

SHE GOT MARRIED LAST YEAR AND QUIT HER JOB...

!?

WAIT A MINUTE...

...BUT MISS TSUKAZAKI...

ば っ

Congruatulations!! Happy Birthday!

THAT'S WHY I...

I DO NOT LIE!

...CAN'T TRUST ANY ADULTS...

...WHO LIE.

IT'S BEEN TWO HOURS ALREADY...

MAYBE HE LEFT...

12 13

OUR FRIENDSHIP IS OVER!

Money!

Money!

Money!

It's like fireworks! I see sparks!

Look, I saw two shooting stars at once!

SHOOTING STARS AND ME PART 2

It was super cool!

Later, someone told me it was the leonids.

I felt like I had seen enough shooting stars to last my entire life.

THREE

There is a book that I used as a resource for the book Kuze-kun is reading in the story.

In this book, the main character is hanging with his girlfriend at the beach and lining up jellyfish. His girlfriend says, "The jellyfish are like rice cakes!"

I read this book when I was in the twelfth grade in high school. I lived in the mountain countryside of Okayama-prefecture and didn't have any chance to see the ocean much. Even though I've never seen a jellyfish and I always dreamt of seeing one with my own eyes one of these days.

To be continued in Volume 4

Jellyfish-Kun

NATSUMI, IT'S DINNER-TIME!

NO THANK YOU.

Um...I gotta poo.

UM...

NATSUMI AND I ARE INVITED TO DR. MORINOMIYA'S SUMMERHOUSE.

THIS IS THE LAST SUMMER VACATION...

...AS AN ELEMENTARY SCHOOL STUDENT.

NATSUMI'S HEAD GOT SO BIG FROM IT, SHE DOES ANYTHING SHE WANTS.

SHE ASKS ME FOR HELP ONLY WHEN SHE'S IN TROUBLE.

Uwaahhan! Asuma, help me!

Again?

THAT'S RIGHT!

WHAT AM I TO HER?

I DON'T WANT TO BE HER CONVENIENT BEST FRIEND ANYMORE!

...I WILL BE A REAL MAN!

DURING THIS SUMMER TRIP...

...I WANT TO BECOME A REAL WOMAN...

DON'T DECIDE WHAT MY GOAL IS WITHOUT ASKING ME.

DR. MORINOMIYA IS TOTALLY HAVING FUN BY TEASING ME...

WHAT WE'RE GONNA D IF NATSUI HEARD OU CONVER- SATION?

It's a secret! Tee hee hee!

THIS...

WHAT IS HER SECRET?

I WONDER IF IT'S SUCH A BIG DEAL?

...SUMMER...

FOUR

CONTINUATION OF SAN (THREE)

After reading the book, I believe that jellyfish is just like a MOCHI (rice-cake). And I still dream of lining up the jellyfish at the beach someday! But my friend recently said to me, "Jellyfish will sting you, so you can't really touch them"

✿ ✿ 🍎

Is this true? Does anyone know the truth? Are you serious?!

It's like MOCHI.

A ha ha ha ha!

A ha ha ha ha!

What I want to do →

How about the people who live around the beach? Have you ever lined up jellyfish at the beach?

OH MY!

WOW, ARE YOU SERIOUS?

WOWWWW!!!

XXX MEANS DOING AND O?

IS IT OKAY TO READ SUCH A THING? NO WAY!

UWWAAH!

I'VE GOT TO TAKE THIS CHANCE!

YOU...

...LOOK PRETTY IN THE BIKINI...

AS IF... IT WERE MADE FOR YOU...

...NATSUMI!

ガはっ

ほっ

RULE OF LOVE NUMBER 20!

GIVE A LOT OF COMPLIMENTS TO THE GIRL YOU LIKE!

You look so pretty in the dress! As if it were made for you, Nana!

Really?

NANA

KEN

←

I DON'T HAVE TIME TO THINK!

SO...

WHAT ARE YOU GOING TO DO NOW?

SAY SOMETHING!

YOU'RE TOO CAUGHT UP WITH WHAT'S WRITTEN IN THE BOOK...

...AND YOU DIDN'T THINK OF HOW NATSUMI FEELS...

...OR HOW YOU FEEL...

Hey!

THE MOST IMPORTANT THING IS HOW YOU BOTH FEEL ABOUT EACH OTHER!

JERK!

YE... YES.

DID YOU GET IT?

NATSUM
I AM
SORRY
ABOUT
EARLIER

...I DIDN'T
MEAN ANY-
THING BAD...

ABOU
WHAT
HAP-
PENE
EAR-
LIER..

PROMISE.

I
JUST
WANTED
TO
BE CLOSER
TO
YOU.

IT'S
SO
BEAUTIFUL!

LIKE THIS...

...MY LAST SUMMER VACATION AS AN ELEMENTARY SCHOOL STUDENT IS ENDING.

BUT... WHEN I COME BACK HERE NEXT TIME...

...FOR SURE...

YES, TOGETHER!

...WITH NAT-SUMI...

YOU MUST BE THINKING ABOUT GIRLS AGAIN!

IT HURTS! WHY THE HECK DID YOU HIT ME?!

OOOPS!

YOU'VE GOT A BLOODY NOSE!

HEY, YOU!

YOU GET EXCITED TOO EASILY, YOUNG BOY!

DR. MORI-NOMIYA, LET'S GO WITHOUT HIM!

UGH!

YOU, PLAY-ER!

THIS STORY WAS PUBLISHED IN MAGAZINE "NAKAY SHI" IN SEPTEMBER 2001

THE NEXT VOLUME WILL BE THE LAST
VOLUME OF "INSTANT TEEN."
I GET MANY FAN LETTERS ASKING ME
TO PLEASE MAKE ASUMA AN ADULT,
TOO! WELL, YOU WON'T KNOW IF HE'LL
GET THE CHANCE OR NOT UNTIL THE
LAST VOLUME. I HOPE I CAN CONCLUDE
THIS STORY NICELY AND MAKE
EVERYBODY HAPPY!

IF YOU WOULD LIKE TO SEND YOUR OPINION OR REQUEST TO ME, HERE IS THE ADDRESS.

TOKYOPOP
5900 WILSHIRE BLVD.
SUITE 2000
LOS ANGELES, CA.
90036

※ ALTHOUGH IT MAY TAKE A WHILE TO GET MY REPLY, I AM TRYING TO WRITE BACK TO ALL MY FAN LETTERS LITTLE BY LITTLE.

★ ★ ★

Did you enjoy the story?

Don't show your ugly face!

See you...

...in the next volume!

Hum hum hum. The rice ball is the best!

Special 👑 Thanks

☑ T. KATADA   ☑ C. MIYASHŌ
☑ S. HIRONAKA   ☑ M. TANABE
☑ A. TAKEGUCHI   ☑ Y. TAKEHARA
☑ M. FUKUSHIMA   ☑ K. KISHIMOTO
☑ I. ZUSHI
☑ My. Friends   ☑ My. Family
2001. 11. 19.   HARUKA. F

TOKYOPOP SHOP

SOKORA REFUGEES

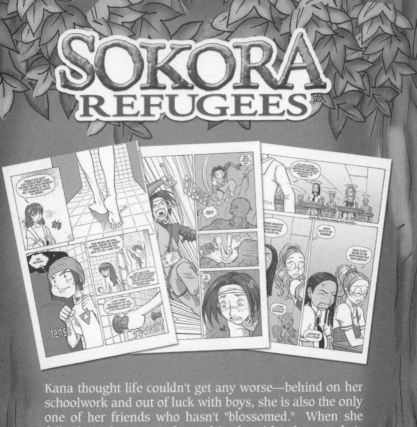

Kana thought life couldn't get any worse—behind on her schoolwork and out of luck with boys, she is also the only one of her friends who hasn't "blossomed." When she falls through a magical portal in the girls' shower, she's transported to the enchanted world of Sokora—wearing nothing but a small robe! Now, on top of landing in this mysterious setting, she finds that her body is beginning to go through some tremendous changes.

Preview the manga at:
www.TOKYOPOP.com/sokora

TEEN
AGE 13+

The savior of a world without hope faces her greatest challenge: Cleavage!

BY MITSUKAZU MIHARA

DOLL

Mitsukazu Mihara's haunting *Doll* uses beautiful androids to examine what it means to be truly human. While the characters in *Doll* are draped in the chic Gothic-Lolita fashions that made Mihara-sensei famous, the themes explored are more universal—all emotions and walks of life have their day in *Doll. Doll* begins as a series of 'one-shot' stories and gradually dovetails into an epic of emotion and intrigue. It's like the *Twilight Zone* meets *Blade Runner!*

~Rob Tokar, Senior Editor

BY MAKOTO YUKIMURA

PLANETES

Makoto Yukimura's profoundly moving and graphically arresting *Planetes* posits a near future where mankind's colonization of space has begun. Young Hachimaki yearns to join this exciting new frontier. Instead, he cleans the glut of orbital junk mankind's initial foray into space produced. He works with Fee, a nicotine-addict beauty with an abrasive edge, and Yuri, a veteran spaceman with a tragic past in search of inner peace. *Planetes* combines the scope of Jules Verne (*Around the World in Eighty Days*) and Robert Heinlein (*Starship Troopers*) with the philosophical wonder of *2001: A Space Odyssey.*

~Luis Reyes, Editor

HYPER POLICE
BY MEE

In a future rife with crime, humans are an endangered species—and monsters have taken over! Natsuki is a cat girl who uses magical powers to enforce the law. However, her greatest threat doesn't come from the criminals. Her partner Sakura, a "nine-tailed" fox, plots to eat Natsuki and gobble up her magic! In this dog-eat-dog world, Natsuki fights to stay on top!

© MEE

LAGOON ENGINE
BY YUKIRU SUGISAKI

From the best-selling creator of *D·N·Angel!*

Yen and Jin are brothers in elementary school—and successors in the Ragun family craft. They are Gakushi, those who battle ghosts and evil spirits known as "Maga" by guessing their true name. As Yen and Jin train to join the family business, the two boys must keep their identities a secret...or risk death!

© Yukiru SUGISAKI

PHD: PHANTASY DEGREE
BY HEE-JOON SON

Sang is a fearlessly spunky young girl who is about to receive one hell of an education...at the Demon School Hades! She's on a mission to enroll into the monsters-only class. However, monster matriculation is not what is truly on her mind—she wants to acquire the fabled "King's Ring" from the fiancée of the chief commander of hell!

© SON HEE-JOON, DAIWON C.I. Inc.

A touching story about a regular guy with an irregular gift.

HANDS OFF!

Girl Gone
Wild West

It's time to teach the boys a lesson...

TOKYOPOP

Girl Got Game♥

Let the games begin...

Crescent Moon

From the dark side
of the moon comes
a shining new star...

T
TEEN
AGE 13+

www.TOKYOPOP.com

When darkness is in your genes,
only love can steal it away.

TOKYOPOP®

D·N·ANGEL

STOP!

This is the back of the book.
You wouldn't want to spoil a great ending!

This book is printed "manga-style," in the authentic Japanese right-to-left format. Since none of the artwork has been flipped or altered, readers get to experience the story just as the creator intended. You've been asking for it, so TOKYOPOP® delivered: authentic, hot-off-the-press, and far more fun!

DIRECTIONS

If this is your first time reading manga-style, here's a quick guide to help you understand how it works.

It's easy... just start in the top right panel and follow the numbers. Have fun, and look for more 100% authentic manga from TOKYOPOP®!